How to make money writing

JANE JOHN-NWANKWO

Jane John-Nwankwo

How to make money writing

Copyright © 2014 by Jane John-Nwankwo.

ISBN-13: 978-1497487147

ISBN-10: 1497487145

Printed in the United States of America

Dedication

Dedicated to all who love writing but don't know the

jewel in their hands.

OTHER TITLES FROM THE SAME AUTHOR:

1. Hightime you made a move!

2. Accept challenges

3. Never be intimidated

4. Design your own methods to navigate

5. Success is for the ready

6. How to market a website

7. How to start your own business

8. How to make money online with no money

Have you bought these books?

THE ART OF WRITING WILL

LAST FOREVER. EVEN IN

HEAVEN, WE ARE TOLD,

THERE ARE BOOKS.

-Jane John-Nwankwo

How to make money writing

Introduction:

An example of a business that one can start from home is writing. I am writing this book lying down on my bed with my computer tilted on my laps for balance. If I sell 50 copies of this book a month and make a profit of $2.78c on each book, that would be $139 a month from one book without my sweating about it because I only wrote the book once, but the sales continue month after month. Remember, I have written many books and I am still writing. So, let's say that in total, I sell 1,000 copies of all my books combined, with $2.78 profit on each copy every month (and I do make up to $10 per book on some), you do the math of how much my work at home job could give me every month. In the writing business, I do not need a receptionist or an office to rent. I just need my computer, my brain and self-discipline. You can see all my books at my website: www.janejohn-nwankwo.com

CHAPTER ONE: REQUIRED

ATTRIBUTES OF A WRITER

While you are in a hurry to know how to make big money writing, I cannot skip this section. Every writer must have the attributes listed below.

Talent: While some people are naturally gifted, some people have to develop themselves by learning and practicing writing skills, and even when we feel we've reached some sort of a pinnacle, we have to keep on improving. I am sure that many readers of this book will be at different stages of their writing development, but these words apply to everyone.

All good writers recognize the fact that they're constantly learning and evolving, and they aren't ashamed to admit it. In fact, no matter how good you think you are, or how good others think you are, put the ego aside and keep learning

and soon you will become an expert in this field.

Commitment: To be a successful writer, you have to

display commitment to the cause. That is, you have to want

to write and complete whatever it is you started. It's all too

easy to write a single paragraph and give up. They key is to

treat your writing as a business. I was making peanuts from

writing until I started treating it as a business.

When you treat your writing as a business, you

must have business hours (hours allocated to writing), you

must have a budget for your business (No matter how

small). This budget will go to advertising your book,

designing professional book covers, editing, etc.

If you do not have any budget at all, don't worry, you may

still make sales, but the difference is too big between when

you advertise and when you don't. Think about it, how can

people buy your product when they don't know it even

exists?

Thousands of writers start writing books they never finish. Please, because you have bought this book, DO NOT be part of the 'Almost Authors'. Commit to the writing business and you will be happy to say "I am a published author".

Writers who stay on the course and earn money do so because they don't shirk hard work; they gain enormous satisfaction from submitting a piece that is the best work they can produce.

The road to the top can be long and hard, but don't let that put you off, as there are many moments to enjoy along the way as well as many opportunities to make money from your craft as you learn. I am a testimony that writing pays off, so let that encourage you whenever you wish to give up. Simply email me at support@janejohn-nwankwo.com. Tell me you read this book and I will offer any advice I may have on writing.

If your English writing is not so good, you may have to use an editor each time, so that your work is a little bit professional. I am not asking for an excellent work. As far as I am concerned, there is no perfect book.

It doesn't matter what you write, just pick a topic and do it. And when you've done it, do it again, but differently. Because without persistence, you won't get anywhere, and if you can't be bothered to spend time improving your art, you won't succeed.

I will discuss about choosing your topic later in this book.

Motivation: Motivation can be difficult for a new writer. Some people's motivation fail because their books did not sell. Let me tell you that you need to see yourself as an information marketer. Don't just write because you want to write. Do write because people need the information you are writing about. I wrote a book on how to make money on poetry and I just sold the first copy few days ago after many months. Why? Because people are not interested in that information. Like every other business, writing is a business that can be unsuccessful if you do not have the right guide. If you follow the principles in this book, you will succeed.

When you sit down to write, it's just you, your computer and your ideas. When you hit a writer's block or your plot doesn't seem to be panning out the way it should, it can be hard to keep going. The best thing you need to do at that time is to take a break and come back to your writing later.

Fortunately for me, I don't usually hit a writer's block. I actually have to discipline myself to go to bed, or say 'This is enough information on this book" or remind myself that it is time to pick my children from school or time to take care of other important things.

If you have a partner who is willing to respect your writing time, count yourself very lucky. My husband is a writer too, so he understands when I tell him, I need to finish the flow of thoughts I am writing on before attending to him. But if you don't, consider joining a writing group so you can meet like-minded people face to face. Find a toastmaster's group in your area. Check Meetup.com or eventbrite.com, or simply search for speaker groups on search engines for your local area. You will find one. I recently found one surprisingly about 6 miles from my house and we meet 7pm to 8:30pm once a week.

If you cannot find a live meeting, join one of the many writers' groups that are available on the Internet. You'll soon find a friendly face and start new friendships that will help you through those tricky times. Sharing writing problems and having someone else read your work and make constructive criticism is a great way to learn and improve what you do.

Organization

A writer has to be organized, and that means having an area where you can write and keep all your paraphernalia within easy reach. You'll be surprised how often you need to reference your dictionary, thesaurus, book of quotations etc. during the course of a session, depending on the genre you are writing.

Furthermore, from day one, set up a filing system on your computer for your digital documents and references as well as one for cuttings, notes etc. in your writing area. The better organized you are, the easier it'll be to lay your hands on what you need, and that will make you feel like writing more, which will result in greater output for you to sell. I am usually working on many different books at a time, so organizing my documents on my computer helps me a great deal.

Planning

Whether you're writing an article, a short story, a novel or an academic paper, before writing one word, plan what you're going to say. It doesn't matter if you're going to write 100 words or 100,000 words, you need a road map to take you from the beginning to the end. It keeps you focused and helps you finish a book much faster than you thought.

If you don't plan, your motivation will be affected and you will experience hindrance in your flow, leading to unorganized pieces of literature that don't sell.

Adaptability: While it may be true that a good article or story is always a good article or story, be aware that the style required by traditional print media is different from that required for online publication. Getting them mixed up can negatively impact your sales, so you need to be clear about the differences.

If you are writing online articles, the writing tends to be more immediate and contain links to further information or related articles and resources. In addition, it contains an element of SEO (Search Engine Optimization) so that the article or story gets picked up by search engines, giving it more visibility and greater worth from the viewpoint of the publisher. And the greater the value to the publisher, the more he or she is likely to pay.

However, don't just litter your piece with SEO terms willy-nilly, as the article is meant first and foremost for human beings and secondly for web bots. Ask the person who commissioned the article if there are any particular words or phrases they want, and work them in naturally.

Also, bear in mind that web-based articles tend to be shorter than those in print and are presented in a more direct way.

With a compelling lead, lots of short paragraphs, subheadings, bullet points and lists, they're easier to read and prolong the attention span of the reader, which is less than that for print media.

CHAPTER TWO:

HOW DO YOU WRITE?

You may be wondering how to start writing. Believe me, it is simple! Do you text? Do you write emails? Then you can do it. The purpose of this book is to spur you into action. I intend each of my books to make a change in the reader's life. So, if you just bought this book just to pass time. Drop it now. It is not for you… (Am waiting). If you did not drop the book, simply follow the guidelines below:

Set a goal: Set an achievable goal. Decide to publish a book within the next 4 weeks.

Choose a topic: What are you passionate about? Do not write a book on what you don't like. Your readers will know, no matter how you pretend.

19

Search your topic: When I decide on what to write, in order to choose a topic that will sell (if it is non-fiction like this book), I usually search on amazon search box to see what people are searching.

This method has helped me in many of my books because I usually start experiencing sales within a few days of publishing and it continues, even before promoting my book. Remember, this method is for non-fiction books like this book. For fiction books, that may not work because, of course people do not search the fake stories going on in your mind.

I wanted to write a book on how to make money, so I went to Amazon search box and started typing "How to make money…" Before I could finish, a lot things popped up. I only saw two things that I was passionate about and could write in a few days. So, I titled my book "How to make money writing".

Decide what type of book: At first, I just wanted to write few pages and make this book an ebook. But after I had a free download promo and saw the number of people interested in my book, I decided to make it both an ebook and a hard copy. Deciding the type of book you want to write will determine the number of pages.

If you want your book to just be an ebook, you can write as little as 10 pages of a book and still make your money. But if you want people to have a hard copy of it, then you definitely need more pages. Deciding the type of book you want to write will also help you to set your goals properly. If you want to publish an ebook on Hawaiian foods recipe, you can do that in one week!

You can also write a short fiction story in one week or even 2 days! More comprehensive books may take weeks to months to accomplish.

That is why I am always working on different books at a time because some of them require longer time to complete while some are vice versa. So, the business keeps going.

What do you want to achieve with this book? :

Answering that question will guide the tone of your book. This book is an informational, motivational as well as a "How to do it" book. My goal is to get my reader to start writing and self- publishing, thus making money after reading this book.

Having this accomplishment in mind guides me in everything I write in this book.

Write Down the outline of the things you want to discuss in your book: Without an outline, you will not produce quality work and you will not be proud of your work because you will keep talking about other things under another topic.

The main outlines will be your chapters. The smaller outlines will be your subtopics.

Start developing the outlines: One outline at a time, start developing and writing down the information you want under each one. By the time you finish writing under the last outline, you just need to read through your work twice. Then you are ready to publish.

If you want to publish on kindle only, simply type kdp.amazon.com on your browser. Don't put "www"Create a password and publish your book. If you wish to publish a hard copy, visit www.createspace.com and publish. Createspace will list your book on Amazon.com, Barnes and Nobles , and other online retailers. You just have to log in once a day or few days a week to see how much you have made on createspace and or kindle. Createspace pays on the 28th day of the month after. Kindle pays 60 days after the month.

CHAPTER THREE

SELLING YOUR BOOKS THROUGH A

SPEAKING CAREER

Many speakers make thousands of dollars after their speech or seminar through the books they sell. I will use this section to discuss a bit about public speaking.

Find your Niche: When an individual wants to go into public speaking as a career, it is important to sit down and find your niche. What am I passionate about? What can I give specific information about very easily? I would not imagine a speaker speaking about a topic they don't like, then you will not speak with authority and this will somehow show through your audience and they will discover that you are not an expert in that area.

I love speaking to new entrepreneurs and motivating them about staying in business and succeeding if they apply certain principles. I draw examples from the few businesses I have, the mistakes I made, and the strategies that worked. Knowing that I am speaking from experience and they see what I am saying, not as fables, but as realities, I guess, helps in the referrals I get.

Solve a problem: Do not be like me when I was starting the speaking business and choose a topic that does not sell. I love poetry so much. I have written so many poems, so I was very ready to tell the world about poetry. To my utmost disappointment, this idea did not sell. While finding your niche and the area you wish to speak about, make sure you are solving a problem. People will pay to find a solution to their problem.

If your speeches do not solve a problem, you will not succeed; successful niches include motivational speaking for different categories of people, organizing seminars for organizations, etc.

Obtain a CEP : If you choose just speeches and no seminar, you do not need a CEP. But if you choose to go the seminar route, it is helpful to obtain a continuous education provider number. You are targeting customers who need continuous education units, for example, I do conduct seminars for healthcare providers (HCP), and most HCPs would be happy to attend my seminars because it helps them to meet the legal requirements of renewing their licenses. This helps to market my seminars. Many a time, since people know that I have different continuous education provider numbers, they call to ask for the next seminar dates.

Advertise to your specific market: In advertisement, there is something called "Target Market." Target Market is the specific population that you would like to speak to. If you are targeting employees, let's say you want to deliver a seminar on improving customer service, you need to approach owners of organizations and present your package. It is always helpful to find a friend who has few employees, deliver your seminar there first, then have them write you a recommendation letter showcasing your performance.

You can deliver the friend's seminar free of charge, just to get the recommendation letter. Also, have the employees (the seminar attendees) fill out a survey at the conclusion of the seminar, collect them and use copies of them when approaching organizations that would like you to speak for them.

Write books on your topic: There is so much credibility when people know that you are not just a speaker, but an author. You have spent your time researching on your niche, and then written books on them. Charge enough for your seminars so that you can give away free copies of your books during the seminar. This makes the participants feel as if they received more than the worth of their money. So, the trick is: don't announce that you are going to give out the books, let it be a surprise.

While in the seminar, take time to advertise your other books and have them ready for purchase at the end of the seminar. Many speakers make more money from their books, than from the speaking engagement. If you were paid $2500 to deliver a 4-hour seminar, and you sold 100 copies each of 3 other books you have published at $20 each, that would be $6000 extra. Make sure you have a way that people can pay with their cards on the spot, like a card swiper on the phone, etc. in the case they do not have cash. **Do not be the one selling your books:** Let the individual you have hired to sell your books be the one selling the books. You should stand by the area because those who enjoyed your speech maybe looking for you to see if you can speak for them at another occasion. Now, imagine if you were the one selling the books, you would not have time to speak to people and you might miss out on referrals. Hiring someone to sell your book is easy, simply type "event staffing agencies" on google. You will see very many of them. Find someone to help in your event.

If you have any questions about any of these strategies, feel free to email me at support@janejohn-nwankwo.com. I will answer your questions for free. That is your bonus for purchasing my book.

Leave Remembrance at any seminar: Make sure to use custom made folders that has your picture on it or your business card on regular manila folders.

Have your audience put their seminar materials in the folders. Your contact number has to be on the folders, so that people can easily contact you or refer people to you.

The Qualities of a Public Speaker : There is a universe of distinction between a public speaker and an incredible public speaker. A public speaker finishes the employment in any case, however an incredible public speaker finishes the occupation in style, with class and with a touch of artfulness. You have to realize what divides the youngsters from the grown-ups and work at joining them into your presentations.

Knowledge - A speaker can discuss anything so long as he or she knows what to say. This is not to say that expert speakers ought not to strive to cut a corner for themselves so they will walk the street to turning into a dominant presence in their line of work. Each public speaker must learn, as the embodiment of public speaking is in having the ability to add worth to your audience and this is done by imparting needed knowledge to them. Spend time in research on your speech and include current examples.

The right language - The sign of an incredible speaker is the capability to have a great charge of a specific language or mode of communication so as to have the capacity to convey information adequately. It is not a necessity that a speaker be a multilingual (that is somebody who comprehends and conceivably speaks different languages).

What is important is that your particular audience understands what you are talking about and are carried along well.

That is to say that if you are speaking to the youth, you need to know the choice of language, while the choice of language is different if you are speaking to old people.

The terms you will use while addressing nurses will differ from the terms you will use while addressing lawyers.

Charisma - This is a common trait that is a key for speakers to have, as it is important in determining if your audience will tune off their minds from you or remain attentive and hear every word you have to say. It is the indefinable attractive energy of fascination that simply makes individuals need to hear you out. The downside of this is that, as a speaker when you depend just on appeal to pass your message crosswise over you will wind up making a disgraceful or empty presentation since the incredible public speaker is one whose presentation is high on rationale, feeling and genuineness or accuracy of information.

Whether you are an experienced speaker, or just starting out, the following points would be helpful in your career:

1. Know Your Audience. To whom will you be talking to? Why are they there? What are they anticipating from you? The replies to those inquiries will impact what a speaker would say. Comprehending the crowd is central to having the capacity to viably tailor and afterward convey a discourse that will be compelling.

2. Know Your Subject. You have been asked to speak in light of the fact that you are an authority on your topic. The crowd will develop confidence in you from the onset of your speech depending on the certainty and authority you show in the conveyance of your material.

Take a breather to refine your subject and mastermind it in the most sensible, unambiguous movement.

Use appropriate language that the audience can easily comprehend, and internalize. PREPARE YOUR SPEECH! I usually rehearse my speech about 2 times to be very prepared.

3. Look and Act Like You Belong. Dress for the event in suitable, well-fitting garments. Be mindful of your carriage and abstain from slumping or inclining toward the platform. Talking in satisfying, conversational tones, being loose and sure, and supporting exceptional eye contact are immeasurable paramounts.

Public speaking is an execution, thus, practice time is important to improve the force of your words, as well as the non-verbal communication and generally speaking visual impact which will help to fortify your message.

It is best to practice before the mirror and time yourself, so that you will determine the duration of your speech and the quality. You can video yourself with your phone and listen to it, as if you were the listener.

4. Pace Yourself. You're not a sprinter dashing wildly at the completion line. The gathering of people will never have an opportunity to make up for lost time if the pace is excessively excited. Furthermore assuming that they can't make up for lost time, they'll surrender. Rather, discover regular stops to permit the vital focuses to be assimilated. Excitement and energy from a speaker are constantly favored, and can additionally serve to enhance more understanding that may generally have a tendency to expand the rate of discourse. The utilization of suitable and decently timed amusement can put both the gathering of people and speaker calm.

5. Make the Connection- Successful speakers are persuading. They persuade others by the force of their own conviction. They are enthusiastic. They cherish their subject. They reach and utilize hand signals and facial declarations that add extra composition to their message. Their words are legitimate and powerful. What's more frequently they use gentle cleverness to furnish a great adjustment to their message.

CHAPTER 4

MAKING THE MOST OF KINDLE

Kindle Promo Days.

Honestly, I was making peanuts on Kindle until I started

making good use of the promo days. It was just like a

miracle. My sales changed drastically! Kindle promotion

days are days that the author allows the readers to

download his or her book for free. This is a great way to

allow your book to be known. It does not cost you

anything. When people know about your book, they spread

the word. It usually works after 2 to 4 weeks. I guess that is

the time they read it, and spread the word, then you start

seeing sales in both your kindle book and your hard copy if

the book is also in hard   copy.

How exactly should you make the most use of your promo days? The key is to announce it at least 7 days before.

These are the lists of websites you can submit your book to announce your upcoming promo days:

Some sites ask that you have at least 5 reviews on the book, others specify no erotica, check out the details before you start submitting your books.

If it seems like a lot of work check out Fiverr.com and pay someone $5 to do it for you. You can often find someone who'll submit your book to free websites or submit press releases for you.

Websites for free book giveaways

These sites can be done in advance of your free days, although some will only allow you to list them if they are currently free.

1. http://www.pixelofink.com/sfkb/
2. http://bargainebookhunter.com/feature-your-book/
3. http://ereadernewstoday.com/category/free-kindle-books/
4. http://www.freebookdude.com/p/list-your-free-book.html
5. http://authormarketingclub.com/members/submit-your-book/ (you have to be a member, but membership is free)
6. http://blog.booksontheknob.org/p/about-this-blog-and-contact-info.html
7. http://www.freebooksy.com/editorial-submissions
8. http://www.thatbookplace.com/free-promo-submissions/
9. http://snickslist.com/books/place-ad/
10. http://addictedtoebooks.com/submission
11. http://www.kindleboards.com/free-book-promo/
12. http://indiebookoftheday.com/authors/free-on-kindle-listing/
13. http://www.ebooklister.net/submit.php
14. http://digitalbooktoday.com/12-top-100-submit-your-free-book-to-be-included-on-this-list/
15. http://thedigitalinkspot.blogspot.com.es/p/contact-us.html
16. http://freekindlefiction.blogspot.co.uk/p/tell-us-about-free-books.html
17. http://www.freeebooksdaily.com/

18. http://www.freebookshub.com/authors/
19. http://www.kboards.com/index.php/topic,97167.0/
20. http://www.frugal-freebies.com/
21. http://www.ereaderiq.com/about/
22. http://freekindlefiction.blogspot.co.uk/
23. http://www.mobileread.com/forums/ (membership required)
24. http://flurriesofwords.blogspot.co.uk/
25. http://askdavid.com/free-book-promotion
26. http://digitalbooktoday.com/join-our-team/
27. http://ebookshabit.com/about-us/
28. http://www.ereaderperks.com/about/
29. http://thefrugalereader.wufoo.com/forms/frugal-freebie-submissions/
30. http://www.goodkindles.net/p/why-should-i-submit-my-book-here.html
31. http://www.blackcaviar-bookclub.com/free-book-promotion.html#.UXFB27XYeOc
32. http://www.totallyfreestuff.com/
33. http://www.icravefreebies.com/contact/
34. http://uk.hundredzeros.com/
35. http://freedigitalreads.com/

Facebook works best when the book is free. Groups

appreciate it if you go back

after your free download day and let them know how it

worked for you and to thank them for their help.

1. https://www.facebook.com/downloadsfreeebooks?fi
   lter=2

2. https://www.facebook.com/FreeEngineeringEbooks
   Since2008

Press Releases

Press releases work best when backed up with a PR

person making calls and generating conversations around

your books. Free press release sites can work just as well

for you, provided you tailor the press releases and they

have an interesting hook and story. Remember

to contact your local newspapers as well as online press

release sites. See some examples below:

1. http://newslink.org
2. http://www.marketwire.com
3. http://www.prnewswire.com

Jane John-Nwankwo

4. http://www.newswire.ca/en/index
5. http://www.prweb.com
6. http://businesswire.com
7. http://www.pr-inside.com
8. http://24-7pressrelease.com
9. http://www.pr.com
10. http://www.mediapost.com
11. http://www.tmcnet.com
12. http://us.cision.com
13. http://www.newswiretoday.com
14. http://www.prlog.org
15. http://pressreleasenetwork.com/index.html
16. http://betanews.com
17. http://www.promotionworld.com
18. http://clickpress.com
19. http://www.businessportal24.com/en
20. http://www.webnewswire.com
21. http://www.przoom.com
22. http://urlwire.com
23. http://groupweb.com

Kindle Countdown Deals

Kindle Countdown Deals is a KDP Select benefit that lets authors provide readers with limited-time discount promotions on their books available on Amazon.com and Amazon.co.uk. It's a great opportunity to earn more royalties and increase discoverability of one's e- book.

Customers will see the regular price and the promotional price on the book's detail page, as well as a countdown clock showing how much time is left at the promotional price. You'll also continue to earn your selected royalty rate on each sale during the promotion.

Here are some of the benefits of Kindle Countdown Deals:

1) **They're time-based**: Not only does this give you more control to decide how long the book is

discounted, but the time remaining for the promotion is visible to customers to increase excitement for the price discount.

2) **Customers see the regular price**: It's easy for customers to see the great deal they're getting, as the regular price is included on the book's detail page, right beside the promotional price.

3) **Royalty rate is retained at lower prices**: You will earn royalties based on your regular royalty rate and the promotional price. As a result, if you are using the 70% royalty option, you'll earn 70% even if the price is below $2.99.

4) **There's a dedicated website**: Customers can easily browse active; Kindle Countdown Deals at www.amazon.com/kindlecountdowndeals, providing yet another way for books to be discovered.

5) **You can monitor performance in real-time**: A new KDP report displays sales and royalties at each price

discount side-by-side with pre-promotion performance,

so it's easy to compare.

Make use of the free promotion and the kindle countdown.

.

CHAPTER 5

HOW TO MARKET YOUR BOOK

The modern world is very connected. The ancient days of authors being an elite club are over. Instead, the world is turning towards the internet. Here everyone can be heard and the world can decide which authors are worth listening to. A large part of this, however, is getting out there to your audience. Marketing your book is essential to every author's success whether her work is digital or hardcopy. Each book presents its own challenges. Each author must be determined and dedicated. The effort is rewarding and will expand your audience. The fact is that if you do not market your book, be ready to make peanuts from your book. You have to treat book publishing as a business. That is the only way to make money in writing!

There are countless ways to market your books whether they are digital or hardcopies. In fact, much of the marketing can crossover between ebooks and hardcopies. The most important thing to remember is to be creative. Think outside of the box. People remember marketing strategies that are unique. As you read these tips, consider how you might expand on the ideas and make them your own.

You must begin by developing a marketing plan. Your marketing plan is your map to becoming successful. It is essential for both digital and hardcopy books. Begin by creating short-term and long-term goals, then writing down the ways that you plan to get there. This is going to ensure that you stay on track and complete all of your tasks. You can always modify your plan as needed, but a basic plan is a must for your success.

5 Ways to Market your Ebook

1. *Be Seen*

A blog or a website is essential for every author. It is especially true for the digital author. Your ebook audience is already tech-savvy. They will want to know who you are and what you are about. A blog or a website will introduce you and your works to the world. Of course, you must make a great impression on your site. Take your time and develop your site. You only get one chance to make an impression and in the digital world, people decide about you based on your online presence.

Use your website or blog to share excerpts of your works and develop a following. It will be a place where people can learn about you and see which works they may be interested in. It also can be a place to share a calendar for book signings or to share progress on your latest works. Above all, it should become the site that appears in the search engines when people look for you. It is your introduction to the world.

It is a good idea to also use social networking. Here people can follow you and your updates. You will be able to promote your blog or website and make big announcements. You will also be able to network with other authors or book clubs in your area. These people can share your announcements or statuses on their sites and will be the first people to publish your reviews. These people will be your word of mouth. They will be the first ones to read your works and the first ones to share. Creating a blog will not cost you a dime. Simply visit www.blogger.com The good thing is that you can also make money from your blogs through 'pay per click' ads, while still introducing yourself. You can visit my blog at janejohn-nwankwo.blogspot.com My blog is different from my website which is www.janejohn-nwankwo.com You need to be seen in order to sell.

Let me give you tips on how to market a website. When you market the website you have opened for your book, you will see sales.

How to market your website

Someone said that having a business without advertising is like smiling to someone in the dark. See it this way: when you open a website, it is only you that knows that you have a website, and of course, you do not want to buy from yourself. Here are a few ways that I have used to market my websites with success. Ask me how many websites I have, the answer is that honestly, I do not know. Some websites, I even forget I opened them until I receive a sale from there. My method is: open a website, do everything to get the word out and be patient to let my new website mature, at least 6 weeks. Then the results will start.

Press Releases: This is a powerful way of advertising websites. I usually use www.free-press-release.com I type up a press release. Don't start asking "what is a press release?" It is simply good information about your business, at least 500 words. Then I log into this website and post my press release. I use the method that allows me to insert links to my website. That costs about $30. I know that is more effective because people can easily click and go to my website and know more about my business, sign up, buy a product, etc.

The free option is good, but with less success because it has a place for the owner of the press release to be contacted. It also has your website pasted. But the individual is expected to paste your website to his browser and then visit your website. Believe me, people do not have all this patience. Insert a link to your website and let people click through. Press releases never expire. Write it once, and let it disseminate into many other connected sites to it.

Social Marketing: Facebook and twitter posts have been said to show much success. Different people have reported varies types of successes. The success I have with facebook is that when people search me or my product, because facebook has a high search engine optimization (SEO), it pops up on the first pages of search engines and people can visit my facebook page on that product and contact me from there. I usually create different websites for my different products to market them. Blog also play this role. Visit www.blogger.com

Forums: Posting in forums is another power tool that works. Visit fiverr.com and search for: "forum posts" . Buy the gigs and let people post your website in forums for you.

Classifieds: Posting in classified has worked well for me. I use mostly Craigslist.com and ebay classified ads. Just type in www.kijiji.com It is the same thing as ebay classified ads. I do get a lot of responses from my ads there. It is free. That is what makes it cool. Ebay classified does not allow you to insert links to your website but it has a prominent button for someone to contact you. To insert a link to your ad on craigslist, use this html code:

<a href="http://www.yourwebsite.com/">Click here for more information!</a>

Insert your website here   Type your text here

When you finish and publish your ad, the link will be clickable to your website.

Backlinks: Backlinks are a great way to increase your web presence. It is contributes immensely to search engine optimization (SEO). It is advisable to create at least 10,000 backlinks for each of your websites.

The more backlinks, the more visible your website will be.

Fiverr.com has gigs for this. But you have to wait for at

least 6 to 8 weeks to see the effect.

Pay per click: Pay per click is a very expensive way to

advertise your website. It is very effective but you may lose

a lot of money. I use google adwords to advertise for one of

my products that costs $999 per product. It is only an add-

on to other methods I have listed above. If you wish to use

this method, simply type: **adwords.google**.com sign up

and create your ad. Make sure to use the method that you

will deposit money into google adwords and your ads will

run from your balance. If you choose the option that google

takes money directly from your bank account, you may

regret it.

Search Engine Optimization: Much of SEO is done while building the website. Most website templates will guide you on how to enable your website be easily found on google. Some of those factors are that you need to devote pages to what your products are, You need to include several times the phrases that people would search on the search engines to find your website. I usually devote certain pages to post those phrases, then I will make the page hidden from the public. But it is on the website and it adds to its visibility.

So, I could open a page and name it SEO, SEO1, SEO2, etc. Then I will paste phrases like:

"Caregiver certification online, online caregiver course, caregiver training online, caregiver course"

I will then copy and paste it over and over until it fills the whole page. Then I will mark the page as hidden.

It is important to know that people you are advertising your websites to are already online searching, so it is good to make things easy for the searchers to locate you and buy your products.

2. *Create a Hype*

Build up to your book release. Doing this gets people excited about the big release day. Do this by including them in the process of releasing the book as well as releasing snippets of your book on your blog or website. This both gets the readers interested and includes them in your triumphs and struggles leading up to the release. The hype will get your fans excited. It keeps you on their radar when preparing for your release. It also keeps people talking and helping spread the word. It gives you momentum as well. Sometimes it can be difficult to wade through all of the pre-release work.

It sometimes feels like wading through peanut butter.

Creating hype gives you the extra push to get you through the final stretch between writing and release. Creating hype will also remind people about when your release is. It will encourage people to buy your book as soon as it comes out boosting your initial sales.

Another way to create hype is to hold a release party. It is a celebration for you and your fans, and it helps to mark your release date with something memorable. It celebrates your accomplishment in a special way with your fans, friends, and family. Be sure to commemorate your releases with specials for your followers. It creates a buzz and gets people excited about your works. The release party also allows fans to buy early signed copies of your book. You will be surprised at how many people get excited about release parties and make an effort to reserve spots at your release parties. The release parties are just as exciting for you as they are for your fans.

If you do not want release parties as I don't, still let as many people as possible to know about your new book. Please refer back to the websites I listed earlier in this book to announce your book. Check page 38.

3. *Use Promotions and Contests*

Promotions are a great way to spread the word about your books. People always love a deal. Most people will even risk a few dollars to try something new. This increases your sales and your ranking on the seller's list. I always do a free kindle download promotion for all my books. It is a great way to gain followers and reviews.

Let me mention that I feel that part of my success in publishing is that I have written multiple books and I am still writing. I feel when people buy one of my books and they love it, they search for other titles from me because people will purchase multiple books from authors that they love.

If a person loves your first book that they downloaded for free, they are very likely to get a hardcopy of it and even buy more copies of your other titles.

Contests are another great way to gain readers. Many people will enter a contest just for a chance to win a prize. This can lead to book purchases from those who did not win the contest, and reviews from both entrants and winners. It also is a fun way to get your name out there. As people get to know you they begin to trust you and spread the word about your writing. It often takes a while to gain reviews and develop a following, but the effort is worth it. It can mean the difference between people knowing your name and you being just another self-publisher.

4. *Get Reviewed*

Reviews consist of a bit more than the reviews on Amazon or other book purchasing sites. There are whole blogs out there dedicated to reviewing books.

It is essential that you send review copies of your book to these book reviewers. They are a trusted source of book knowledge.

One review on a trusted blog can change your entire career as an author. A solid review on one of these sites will bring a quick increase in sales and many lifetime followers.

Bloggers aren't the only people who can spread the word about your works. Media releases, zines, and newsletters are all great ways to get your information out there. The more people that review your work, the better known your works become. In this world, name recognition is essential for success. Reviews are a way to establish your name and your book titles. Try to start with twenty Amazon reviews. Twenty reviews will establish your name and give you a good solid start to your ebook marketing.

Reviews and blogs will be what keeps your book in the public eye. It will help potential readers from that first opinion of your book, and eventually helps them decide to purchase and read your book.

5. Network on Amazon

Amazon has several very good options for its authors.

Firstly, Amazon reviews are invaluable. Many people trust the reviews on Amazon when making purchasing decisions. Have people read your book and write reviews for you. The reviews need to be honest and genuine, but your book club, network, friends, or family, should all be able to help with this.

You may also want to consider contacting Amazon's top reviewers to see if they are willing to read a proof of your book. These Amazon reviewers are the Amazon elite when it comes to reviews.

These people have written enough reviews that they are trusted and respected by sellers and buyers alike. Many of them may not respond, but one or two reviews from a top reviewer will greatly help your book.

You can also buy reviews from websites like www.paidbookreviews.org, www.getbookreviews.org, www.payforbookreviews.com, www.paidbookreviewservices.com

I suggest when using these sites, you tell them to write what they feel about your book, that way, you will see different stars under your book. There must be something bad your book, and a lot of things good.

Some bad reviews help, while some are just from your competitors. I never knew that people post negative reviews on their competitors' books until someone asked me if I wanted him to post negative reviews on my competitors' books.

I rejected that, because that is against my belief. So, after that incident, I started to read some reviews with a broader mind and I began noticing that a few of my reviews are as a result of sheer jealousy of publishing success.

Therefore, do not be hesitant to buying reviews to boost your book sales.

Also, get involved in the Amazon forums. There are a few forums that provide Q&A sections for authors. There are also forums about publishing and promoting books. These are simply other places to go to promote your work and get your name out to potential readers.

Promoting an ebook can be fun, but it can also be difficult. The downside is that you may or may not see people face to face. The upside is that you can reach so many people on the different parts of the world.

As with hardcopies, it is important to stick with it and stay focused. It can often be daunting to work for virtual rewards, but the hard work will won't be for naught. With a good work ethic and perseverance you too can have a successfully ebook on the virtual market.

Ebooks can leave an author feeling a bit disconnected from fans, but they are a significant source of revenue and a significant source of fans and followers. Keep working on the ebook and you will see results.

Helpful Sites:

http://www.huffingtonpost.com/fauzia-burke/ways-to-promote-your-ebook_b_3963836.html

http://www.createmagazines.com/article-posts/tips-to-boost-ebook-sales/

http://www.yourwriterplatform.com/promote-and-market-your-book/

5 Ways to Market your Hardcopy book

As I said earlier, when you advertise your e-books, it cuts across your hard copies of the same title. In spite of this being in the digital age, many people still prefer to read hardcopies of books.

There's just something comforting about curling up with an actual book.

There is something familiar about the smell and the feel of a physical book. There is something that draws us all to an overstuffed chair in front of a fireplace with a book. It's so much more fun to hide under the blankets with a flashlight whilst reading a horror story than it is to hide under a blanket with a tablet. We all love technology, but hard copy books are still popular. This means that you must work hard to market your hardcopies too.

Jane John-Nwankwo

In addition to the strategies listed above, marketing your

hardcopy book will take a little more physical effort than

marketing your e-book. Physical books may require

marketing your book in person to bookstore, speaking at

events, meeting book clubs, and meeting local bookstore

managers.

 Physical books require a lot more face to face interactions,

but it is just as rewarding.

There is a significant market for hardcopies of books, and

hardcopy sales can be a significant way to increase your

revenues and get your name out there. It requires

perseverance and commitment, but it is still an integral part

of being a published author.

Books are Judged by Covers

People say not to judge books by covers, but we all know that one of the most important parts of the book is the cover. We learn so much about the book by looking at the cover.

That being said, it is important to have a professional cover that is pleasing to the eye. It is a great idea to have several covers drawn up to choose from. You can get professional book covers at :

www.fiverr.com

Even if you use createspace to publish, it is always good to get professional book covers and download it into the createspace bookcover template.

The cover is one place that you should spare no expense on. After all, this is your book's first impression. The problem is that your book can't talk. It is entirely up to your book cover to convince people to read.

Additionally, the cover art can both be branding for you and promotional art for your book. This can be used on your site, for networking, or for promotional posters. The artwork will not only be the first impression, it will be the strongest impression. You want the artwork to stand out enough that people will recognize your books by their covers without ever seeing your name. It is a form of branding and it will help you stand out on the market. When choosing a cover, have an artist draw up several possible covers and pick the one that will best fit your book. It is often a good idea to enlist the help of your friends and family in choosing a cover, but the decision is ultimately yours. Just be sure that it is a cover that you can be proud of and that fits the   style and genre of the book.

2. Attend Book Conventions

Book conventions allow you to network with authors, readers, and publishers while getting your name out to readers. You can often rent a table or booth for your books where you can sell and market your book. There are also many classes and meetings to attend that address things such as connecting with publishers and marketing your book. Another perk of being published is that you are qualified to speak at conventions and book clubs.

The classes and meetings will give you a chance to learn new writing techniques and marketing techniques. You will find that you have a chance to explore and expand on your genre.

Others who are in the process of publishing will value your knowledge and your experience. This is yet another way to pique interest in your book, gain followers and readers, and make your name known.

These conventions help you to spread your name and you book titles. It is another way to promote name recognition and allow people to become familiar with your works. Book conventions will not only promote your name and books, but they can give you the resources to improve yourself as an author.

3. Spread Your Works to your Community

Communities love having local authors. They take great pride in supporting local artists, including writers. This means that getting your name out in your community can be a great way to promote sales. Local shops will often agree to carry the works of locals if you ask.

Another great way to promote yourself to the community is to donate copies of your books to local libraries, as is appropriate. Many libraries take donations and even have a section dedicated to local artists.

Many local coffee shops also often promote local artists. You will find that many have bookshelves and will allow you to sell books through that shop. Doing this not only supports other local businesses, but lets you get to know other artists and businesses owners. It develops goodwill in the community and makes your name known to those who live around you.

Getting to know your community both spreads goodwill and promotes name recognition. Both of these are proven marketing tools.

4. Meet the Author

Have a release party. Do a meet and greet. Have a book signing. Do whatever you can to create hype around your book. People get excited about meeting published authors. People love to have signed copies of books. Often people will attend meet and greets or sit through a book reading because people are fascinated with published authors. Personal marketing works well because you make a connection with potential readers. You get a chance to market yourself to people and spread your enthusiasm to others.

When you plan an event, plan to speak or read from your book for about thirty minutes. After that, take questions for another fifteen minutes. This will allow people to get to know you. It makes you seem more personal.

A large part of selling books is connecting with the world around you.

Scheduling meet and greets allows you to connect with potential consumers and encourages them to purchase your book.

5. Use Technology

This book is a hardcopy, but technology is still your best friend. Actually, the success I have had so far in my hardcopies has come 99% from the internet. Use the internet methods I had listed earlier in this chapter. Use networking to release excerpts. Create a Facebook page and a Twitter account for your book to get the word out. Send out newsletters and update blogs. All of this brings your book to the attention of potential readers. Technology lets you encourage your followers to read your book. It keeps them up to date on the status of the hardcopy release.

It allows you to run contests and send signed hardcopies to your fans. The internet isn't just for promoting ebooks. Technology is a great way to promote nearly any product that you need to sell. Books are no exception to this. A good website and some good social networking will take your hardcopy places that you only dreamed of.

It is essential to gain online reviews even for hardcopies. In my experience with Amazon and Barnes and Noble, when a review is written on a version of the book, like e-book, it shows up on the hardcopy too.

Even if your hardcopy does not have an ebook counterpart, reviews will still be the lifeline of your book. Bookstores still exist, but they are having a hard time in the modern economy. Bibliophiles often order their books from websites rather than bookstores.

The hardcopies must have an online presence. Think about the first thing that you do when you hear about a new book. Many people look for information online in order to find out more about both the author and the book. An online presence is essential for all books regardless of its format.

Promoting books can be a little challenging, but it is always worth it No matter what you do, stick with it and don't give up. It requires a great deal of determination and dedication, but anyone who is an author probably already has these qualities. Marketing is the lifeline of your book whether it is an e-book or a hardcopy. Marketing will either make or break your book. Many of the marketing techniques for e-books are applicable for hardcopies and vice versa.

Jane John-Nwankwo

The key to marketing is to be creative, seize available opportunities, and put yourself out there. The process requires time and energy, but the journey is worth it. There is a strong market out there that you have to work to tap into. The world is very plugged in to the internet, but hardcopies will never fall out of fashion. It sometimes seems as if the book market is a slower, more difficult market, but don't give up on the book market.

It is important for you to tap this market and create a niche for yourself in order to be a successful, well rounded author. Just keep going and you will eventually see the rewards. My propelling strength in the book business has been the rewards. As I see my books sell, I know that my effort is not in vain and so, I invest more into the business. After all, who would not invest more into a thriving business?

Resources

http://www.writersdigest.com/editor-blogs/guide-to-literary-agents/how-to-promote-your-book-press-releases-media-pitches-and-promotional-materials

http://www.writersstore.com/15-do-it-yourself-tools-to-promote-your-book/

Chapter 6

Other Writing Opportunities for Money

You can either be a freelancer or work full-time for somebody else.

If you want to work for somebody else, they're most probably going to demand formal qualifications, particularly if you're starting out. They may need samples of your previous work, and may even ask you to submit something as a test of your abilities. If you're more experienced, you'll still have to show them what you can do, although your experience should help ease you through a few doors. Jobs with publishing companies can be found in trade journals, while many other businesses which employ writers advertise in the job sections of newspapers and magazines, or on their own websites.

For freelancers, the market is wide, but very competitive. If you wish to go the freelancing route, simply search for freelancing websites on search engines and make your choice.

Traditional Outlets:

All the traditional outlets are still available – newspapers, magazines and book publishers. They're notoriously difficult to break into, but please don't let that stop you trying. I am not a fan of traditional outlets because I cannot stand having my work turned down just because I did not write according to someone's specifications.

To stand the best chance of success, do your homework on the publication or publisher you want to consider your work, find out their submissions procedure and stick to it like a clam. Whether you agree with it or not does not matter. They have published it for their own reasons and you must adhere to it.

If they ask for your script in Ariel 10, give it to them in Ariel 10 and not in Times New Roman 10. Likewise, be sure to include the information they ask for in your covering letter. While that won't guarantee your work being accepted, it'll get you in through the front door and on to an editor's desk rather than straight into the bin.

Internet Outlets

The good news is that there's always someone somewhere looking for website content. The not so good news is that many website owners are not willing to pay more than a couple of dollars for their content. Try to avoid such sites if possible, as they're hard labor and your work won't be appreciated, but if that's all you can get to start with, it's better than nothing, as it means you're now a professional writer.

Yes, someone has paid you money for your writing! But believe me, that is not the purpose of this book.

I am only including these points to give you more options.

My purpose is to get you into the self-publishing business and start making you full time income right away. Did I say full time income? Yes. Full time income.

Web-based publications

Many print publications also have an Internet arm, so send a polite enquiry, along with links to your best stuff, and ask if they would be interested in your services.

And don't just stop at the obvious names, as there are specialized and niche publications all over, and each one needs filling. Articles on such sites also have a more rapid turnover than those in print, so publishers are always on the lookout for fresh new voices with something different to say.

Listing sites

Sites such as freelancewritinggigs.com and online-writing-jobs.com bring those who require content together with writers in an online equivalent of classified advertising. Some of these sites contain further links to the job opportunities, where you have to apply according to the brief, while others contain jobs that you have to bid for. The problem with those is that it often ends up in a race to the bottom as people who are desperate for work submit ridiculously low bids just to get the work.

To avoid that, consider subscription sites, such as writer-editors.com, which means that only those who pay get to see the jobs. While it's not generally recommended to pay for potential employment, these sites do filter out those who aren't serious.

Pay per click

Pay per click sites allow you to post your article or story, but don't pay you until it has received a minimum number of viewings, or you receive an incredibly low base rate which is topped up over time according to the number of clicks the article receives. While it may be a good way to get your writing from your laptop into a wider sphere, despite claims to the contrary, you aren't going to make any worthwhile money. Think about the time and effort that goes into just one 500-word article and I think you'll agree. I get money from these, an average of $10 a month. Am sure that is not why you bought my book. But it feels good to get a direct deposit from google, anyway.

Content mills

A rather unflattering name, but an apt description of the genre. Sites like textbroker.com and greatcontent.com are a good way to obtain a regular source of income.

Again, you won't get rich, but they provide a steady stream of work, and if you're one of their best writers, you get paid reasonably well.

To progress from one level to another, you have to consistently turn in top-quality work, and they're very fussy about who gets to level 5, as it's their reputation on the line. When you've been allocated a level, you're free to choose to write any article you like that's advertised at that level or below. Articles cover all topics under the sun and vary in length from 50 to 1,000 words plus. Good writers also get asked to join better paid specialized teams. There are many content mills on the Net and they all operate in a similar manner, though with differences regarding pay rates and so forth.

You usually have to register to find the full details, but it's worth taking the time if you wish to go that route. The two sites mentioned are acknowledged as a couple of the better ones, although wisegeek.com and demandmedia.com also have their supporters.

Your own blog/website

Why not start your own blog or website? Choose a theme and start uploading your stuff. For example, if you're into gardening, help others by posting advice and tips, and get others to contribute. How do you get paid? Simple. Decorate your site with advertisements from Google, Amazon and other large companies, then when anyone visits your pages and clicks on an ad, you earn money. But you have to drive traffic to it.

Competitions

If you're a fiction writer, there are hundreds of competitions open every month, all with cash prizes.

Admittedly, you usually have to pay a small entrance fee ($2 – 5), but that goes towards the prize pot, or there wouldn't be a competition in the first place. Most competitions are run by small sites, which don't make money, but operate for fun, so you're not being ripped off when they ask you to pay. However, if you read between the lines, what that tells you is that they don't have many readers (probably in the hundreds), and out of those readers, only a very small percentage enter the competitions, making the chance of winning for those who do enter even greater. It isn't a guaranteed income by any means, but it helps you refine your writing, and the better you get, the more chance you have of winning. A Google search will give you a clue, but one of the most respected sites to list upcoming competitions is jbwb.co.uk.

Academic writing

This can be a big earner if you're specialized in a particular subject and possess at least a first degree, or a diploma. Basically, it's writing essays and other assignments for students. Whether or not you consider that to be morally wrong is up to you, but if you can get past that, there are literally thousands of students all over the world requiring help. Academic ghostwriters make thousands of dollars a month. No wonder many graduates cannot write a simple essay. A Google search will bring up the companies that provide this sort of work, but be wary of those operating from low-wage economies, as they have a reputation of withholding payment.

If you are in the medical profession, this section is a bonus for you. If you are not in the medical field, do not skip this section because you will surely learn something from it.

Medical writer: I am going to start with someone being a medical writer. If you have a flair for creativity or the ability to translate medical components into a simplified language that is easy for the layperson to understand, then transitioning from a nurse working side-by-side with patients to a medical writer is just the career move for you. Your experience working in the healthcare field will put you in a prime position to understand the often complex medical terminology, while your writing skills can help you to write material that is easy for the reader to easily understand.

Your Job Duties: Because medical writing can encompass a wide range of work completed for media, industry, government and pharmaceutical companies, your job duties could vary greatly from one position to the next.

- You may be required to investigate and research findings about new products and new drugs and then prepare documents that will be used to seek approval from the FDA.

- You could find yourself helping physicians with writing their research papers or medical reviews.

- You may work with continuing medical education companies that develop educational materials to help medical professionals prepare for the next phase of continuing their education and furthering their career.

- You could find work writing about new and exciting research developments for medical journals, magazines, newspapers, websites, and other publications that offer a focus on healthcare issues.

Your hands-on experience as a healthcare professional will put you in a great position to understand how the medical and healthcare industry works.

Options for Medical Writer Opportunities

As a healthcare professional with exceptional writing skills you will find yourself very much in demand at a number of companies. Some of the places that you could find yourself working on your way to

accomplishing your goal of earning $100,000 a year include the following.

- Pharmaceutical companies
- Medical software firms
- Medical device manufacturers
- Universities and other continuing education companies
- Clinical research organizations
- Government organizations with a focus on healthcare
- Medical journals
- Medical websites

- Freelance writing

- Authoring books for renowned publishing companies

- Independent publishing (which is one of the things I do)

- Ghostwriting for non-academic papers where the author has the idea of what to write but lacks the writing ability. The price is usually between $20 to $50 for every 250 words (a page). In an 8 hour day, while making your lunch and taking necessary breaks from your home computer, you can type up nothing less than 10 pages. If your charge was $40/page, that would be $400 a day. If you do this 10 days on your days-off in a month, you have $4000 in your hands outside your paycheck. As your name is known and the published authors use you as repeat customers while you are still securing more clients, you can start outsourcing your job to other seasoned writers. Many professional ghostwriters make a minimum of $20,000 a month working from home. Please make sure that your services are not used for academic purposes. A good way to start freelance writing will be enrolling in websites like elance.com and other such sites freelance writing sites, advertising your services under classifieds, writing to medical and nursing journals, etc. Whether you are writing presentations, research papers, or technical manuals for medical devices, there are a number of key skills that you will need to have in order to find success in your new field. You will need to have the ability to translate healthcare studies into an approachable language that is custom-tailored to reach out to the targeted audience. This could involve translating a particular complex medical study into several different versions that are appropriate for healthcare professionals, investors, regulators, or even the general public. There will be need to have good attention to detail, be flawless in your accuracy, have exceptional research skills, and of course possess solid writing talents

Accomplishing Your Goals of $100,000 in 12 Months:

The medical writer is not often thought of as being a lucrative career choice.

But the reality is that an accomplished writer with good credentials as a nurse will be in a position to command a much higher income. You may need to get a few jobs in order to establish yourself as a subject matter expert, but with a good writing portfolio and the drive to succeed in your chosen career, you could easily land yourself into making between $5,000 to $10,000 a month just writing from your computer for different companies, part-time. The average salary for a medical writer in the USA sits at $75,000 but it can easily be improved upon by ensuring that your writing skills are exceptional and that your nursing and medical knowledge skills are without fault. The larger pharmaceutical companies are also often very generous with the salaries they offer to their medical writers. Keeping up with current

medical advances and writing your own editorials for

submission in healthcare publications

are great ways to boost your income. Whether you are

working as a medical writer for the top medical schools in

the country or publishing research articles in notable

medical journals, or even publishing your own books like

you have mine in your hands, you are sure to find out that

being a medical writer is a hugely fulfilling career

opportunity without a paid office.

Conclusion

Whichever market you choose, be it online or offline,

always maintain a professional approach and deliver work

on time. Your reputation will grow, and when people know

they can depend on you, they'll push more work in your

direction.

Remember, too, that websites come and go, so you must keep abreast of what's happening on the Internet in order to make the most of all opportunities. Don't expect immediate success and riches, and you won't be disappointed, but if you keep at it, you **will** make it and then one day may be able to give up the day job.

I strongly suggest you start publishing ebooks of few pages, then grow from there.

ABOUT THE AUTHOR

Jane John-Nwankwo CPT, RN, MSN, PHN is a motivational speaker and published author of more than 45 books which include textbooks for healthcare training, fiction for entertainment, how to start small businesses, and motivational books.
Simply search
"Books by Jane John-Nwankwo"
On Amazon.com, Barnes & Nobles, etc

Visit her website:
www.janejohn-nwankwo.com

Book Jane John-Nwankwo as your motivational speaker

now at www.JaneJohn-Nwankwo.com

With more than 10 years as a professional speaker, Jane John-

Nwankwo can hold any audience sitting straight on their

chairs for any length of time! She is a published author of

more than 45 books including the upcoming "It's in your

hands" (A motivational and inspirational book)

She received her Masters of Science in Nursing from

University of Phoenix, and is currently pursuing a PhD in

Nursing Science from University of Phoenix. Her speaking

interests include: Motivational speeches for new business

owners, Motivational speeches for any category of people,

Employee seminars, Students' Empowerment,

Healthcare topics, Topics related to women, and any Christian

topic. Book a speaking appointment today and become a

repeat customer because of 100% satisfaction.

www.ingramcontent.com/pod-product-compliance
Lightning Source LLC
Chambersburg PA
CBHW051735170526
45167CB00002B/938